Praise
My Body Lives

Megha Sood's first collection *My Body Lives Like a Threat* provokes and inspires. In her powerful voice, the author personalizes the political as in *Transformation, Asphyxiated,* and *A Nation in a Chokehold.* In this collection, bodies are prayers, safe-havens, and an eye of the storm. There is hope in these poems too: "...we expose our deepest and softest parts to heal ... that's how the body learns ..."

— **Maria Lisella,** 2020 Fellow *Academy of American Poets*
and *Queens Poet Laureate*

With its stunning imagery and beautifully crafted lines, *My Body Lives Like Threat* functions like a hand cupping our chins and turning our faces to that which we are too afraid to see alone. The world is difficult and filled with injustice, look. The world is broken and littered with boundaries, violence, and injured dreams. Look, look, do not look away. This is the collection that will build a new city over the bones of decaying patriarchy, and Megha Sood is the poet who will stand in the middle of that city, lantern-lit, leading us, with her words, to a better way.

— **Melissa Studdard,** Poet and Author

Deeply conscious of her location as an immigrant and a woman, Megha Sood creates in *My Body Lives Like a Threat* a conduit for the voices of the vulnerable and oppressed in the United States. Through unrelenting images of pain and suffering, the poems bear witness to the history of brutality against African Americans and other immigrant groups, refusing to numb the pain wrought by injustice, since peace is "the metaphor of denial." Megha's powerful words find their resonance in the pause between language and action, where community and consciousness overcome voices of privilege. Despite the burden of patriarchy and state violence, in Megha's poetry, solace lies with both grief and love.

— **Pramila Venkateswaran,** Author of *The Singer of Alleppey*
and Poet Laureate of Suffolk County, Long Island

Megha Sood weaves stark reality with vibrant images to create a surreal yet sharp understanding of the complexity of humanity. Each piece entices you to the next, drawing you further into the heart of this body of work. Living. Vibrant. Unapologetic. Powerful. Once I started, I couldn't stop reading."

— **Rescue Poetix,** Poet, Author, Performer
and 2021-22 Poet Laureate of Jersey City, New Jersey

Megha Sood's *My Body Lives Like a Threat* is an impassioned and unflinching war cry against racial and gendered violence and oppression. Laced with Dante-esque, vividly visceral imagery, the poet poses a series of potent and compelling questions - *"Does scream have a religion? Do cries have a race? Does hurt have a gender?".* Railing against a catalog of griefs, from deeply personal to global "pain like a stray dog"- the "razor-sharp vernacular of death", "raging inequality" and "a cornrow of failed desires", the poet rebels against "a million slithering tongues" and the "putrid stench of indifference" in a world where systemic suppression "takes the shape of a chokehold". Much as this book is a fervent and unflinching war cry, it is also a cry from the heart, a bloody-knuckled digging for hope.

— **Anne Casey,** Author of *Out of Emptied Cups,*
Award-Winning Poet and Writer

Just to gain a little insight between interstices, I recommend the reader starts with the title poem before being wooed and devoured by Megha's craft's excellent attention to her social justice perspective.

The line that sells the book for me is:
every time I twist my tongue to
shape a word, I mispronounce
your fear
"a new threat is born."

— **Jacquese Armstrong,** Author of *Blues legacy* ©2019,
Winner of the 2019 Naomi Long Madgett Poetry Award

My Body Lives Like a Threat by Megha Sood is a collection of poetry that speaks to the feeling(s) of many people living all over the world. Depending on the country, culture, race or religious orientation of the reader the title

My Body Lives Like a Threat

FLOWERSONG
PRESS

poems by

Megha Sood

FLOWERSONG
PRESS

The Debut Poetry Collection of Megha Sood

by
Thelma T. Reyna, Ph.D.

Today, in the midst of burgeoning technology, pandemia, sociopolitical polarization, and mind-spinning complexity, poetry still holds sway in how we communicate across generations, cultures, class, occupations, ideologies, and continents. Poetry is a "frontliner" in crises, exposing and dissecting naked truths. It is the common man's language and the language of elites. In other words, as it has been since ancient times, poetry is the go-to language of *human beings* in matters of import, at times when common conversation is insufficient to express what swirls in our souls. Thank goodness this is how it's been and how it still is.

Megha Sood is one of these communicators who in recent years has taken up the mantle of telling truth in verse. In this book, *My Body Lives Like a Threat*, her first full-length poetry collection, she peels back layers of complexities in this crazy-quilt life, revealing our world in all its frightening upheavals, yet also in all its affirmation of the unshakable goodness of humanity. Megha Sood's book shows us a world that is literally as well as metaphorically burning. But she also shows us its resilience.

Her journey in creating this book was not pre-ordained but was instead a fate eventually showing itself: circuitous, arduous, and unexpected. She was born in Naya Nangal, Punjab, India, and was raised in Delhi. Her native language is Hindi, and her career was in the technological field. Although she was formally educated in English in India, she was not formally trained in writing poetry, especially poetry in English, which she began doing on her own a mere four years ago. She has now created over 800 English poems, many of which have been published in literary journals, anthologies, reviews, and books across the globe, winning awards and substantial acclaim along the way. She wrote a chapbook—*My Body Is Not an Apology*—published this year by a prominent publisher and already garnering wide praise.

And now we have her full debut collection of 47 poems arranged in five sections encapsulating themes that run like threads through her poetry: Black Truth; War and Peace; My Body Is Not an Apology; A Just Immigration Policy; and My Body Lives Like a Threat. Poetry is not always political; but in Megha's hands, the sociopolitical arena of our lives is the vessel holding her creations. Issues that have eternally plagued civilizations and that still sunder societies are examined, explained, reviled, parsed, and laid bare for us to dwell upon and better understand. She casts her literary net wide, across nations and across decades, proving that sociopolitical issues are universal, and they affect all people with the same pain, fear, reactions, and hopes.

So her book shows us—in her powerful, graphic, clear poetic voice—the ravages of war, the dangers, and cataclysms of immigration, the poignancy of poverty, the brutality of racism, the costs of gender inequality and oppression, the horrors of environmental destruction, the terror of genocide, whether in foreign autocracies or in America...scene by scene, with clear-eyed honesty and precision in the retellings. Megha is the conscience of our people, all the world's peoples, who have suffered the indignities of oppression and deprivation. She does not flinch in recording for society the transgressions we the people have foisted on our fellow human beings and continues to do so, showing how our lesser angels are often entrenched in habits and traditions that defy compassion.

Yet Megha balances her observations of our world with better angels, too, in a voice saturated in optimistic defiance of harsh status quos. In one of her exquisite prose poems, she examines the value and power of humans marching in solidarity against racism and hate, specifically invoking the summer marches in the United States and around the world protesting the murder of George Floyd. Megha writes in "A Revolution by Choice":

> Where the fearless *Athenas* are appearing, speaking power to the truth, brushing shoulders in the protest-laced streets, where we know we can survive if we have enough compassion and empathy to let others survive. Where the collective grief and voices screaming and gasping for breath in a chokehold for 9.29 minutes has now become a war cry for the revolution. Where white silence is counted as abuse. Where privilege is not defined by the color of your skin. Where the man stands witness to his own sins. Where the god's hands are no longer creating a perfect creature but a man of imperfections. When we can see our reflection in the mirror and say to ourselves, *this is the moment that belongs to me*, a change, a revolution that I birth by choice. (p. 20)

Another of Megha's deeply-prized values, individual freedom, is affirmed soundly in her poem, "Path to My Freedom":

My head pointing towards cerulean skies
laced with dreams and equality,
the pain of unspoken truths for generations
still lodged in my throat
I challenge my resolution
the fears of losing seeded deeply.

But I never give up--
as I learned from the footsteps of warriors
the path to my freedom is laced
with the blood of my determination
which their shameful eyes still can't bear to see. (p. 66)

And finally, in "My Survival Story," the poet unleashes her fierce
determination to evolve beyond constraints she has navigated as an immigrant
from a land beset by poverty, hardship, and inequalities. In a heartfelt manifesto,
she commits to reinventing herself by unearthing her "untrammeled beauty
within," and reconstituting the "broken pieces" of her "prosody of pain" as she
continues learning, growing, becoming stronger. In this voice, Megha is the
ultimate warrior woman whose values are entwined throughout this book.

. . . .
Like a sapling breaking
from the blind seed
I'm sprouting, I am thriving.
. . . .
Like a reflection of the summer sun
shining into a million versions of me,
on shards of broken mirror

. . . .
I'm the war cry, the mortal fear
residing behind the enemy lines

. . . .
The broken pieces I foraged together
to make a whole of me
an untrammeled beauty within.

This fecundity is my survival extinct
to handle the plethora of emotions

life throws at me,
Undulating between the proximity and prosody of pain:
I'm learning. Yes, I'm growing. (p. 67)

Megha Sood's book has come full-circle: in the first section, Black Truth, she proclaims: "You tried to ruin me but you turned me into a warrior,/A blind seed ready to branch out." ("Transformation," p. 13). She has spilled her poet's pain and tears throughout the pages of this book, but in the end, we see her as what she pronounced herself on page 16 to be: *a warrior.*

And for that, we are deeply thankful.

Thelma T. Reyna is a national award-winning author of 10 books—a short story collection, 2 chapbooks, 3 full-length poetry collections, and 4 edited anthologies. She is also a former Poet Laureate in California, and Chief Editor/Publisher of Golden Foothills Press in Pasadena, CA.

TABLE OF CONTENTS

My Body Is Not An Apology

A Just Immigration Policy

My Body Lives Like A Threat

For my son, Siddharth,
My shining beacon in every storm

All poets, all writers are political. They either maintain the status quo, or they say, "Something's wrong, let's change it for the better."

— **Sonia Sanchez**

I. Black Truth

Peace - A Metaphor for Denial

Peace, an act of ignorance
an act of denial is not bliss   *no more*
when silence is gutted like a fish
and blood of your own fills the street.

How long can you be the puppet
in your own peaceful country?
this act of abandonment speaks a muted language
for all the hearts trapped like sparrows
on the other side of town.

The wall creates a boundary between me and humanity
they are still considered illegal with one foot in my land
another bloodied and stuck in the barbwire
that I put around God's own country.

I was born with a privilege
to call the piece of the earth my own
No matter it is laced and seeped
with someone's else blood
it belongs to *me* now.

The young boy is   shot
the pavement is stained by the color of his blood
dark and useless;
to the people of this peaceful country.

Those who pull out the armrest and the beach chairs
to see the stars light up the sky
and the deafening noise
muting the wails of a widowed mother.

They sip the beer as cold as their souls,
leaving the scene with a shrug and a short sigh.
Ignorance is bliss. Peace is a *metaphor* for *denial*
in this country, I call mine.

A Nation in a Chokehold

The streets are overcrowded
lanes are bustling with protest
thrumming with anger
overcrowded bus stops, sidewalks, bike lanes, parks
brimming and spilling with pain
Unfettered;
Uncontrolled

Everywhere there is quarantine
where the lanes should be deserted
where everyone should be   *six feet apart*
masks covered mouths but still breathing
with breaths laced with privilege

Here the nation recalls the pain
the unanswered angst of those calling from the grave
for those grieving souls who are yet to be put to rest
those headstones, now a place marker for a black mother
to sit and cry alone in the deep folds of the night

Here the nation mirrors the screams
of the black blood lacing the sidewalks
mouth gaping at the nakedness of the whole nation
staring back at the end of a gun *a police gun*

Here the nation acknowledges the police shooting went awry
here the nation recalls how the protectors devour
here the nation recalls how easy it is for you to forget
a loss of life and wait for the next news cycle to begin

Here the nation recalls how eyes pop out
losing life in an instant:
when your brain misses the next wave
of life-giving air coursing through your veins

Here the nation recalls how the brutal hands
loaded with power thick as greed,
dripping with incessant hunger
took lives boisterously

Here the nation recalls how life was ignored
leaving the warm and supple heart
on the sidewalks pitted with fear and blood
of the beautiful black bodies

Here the nation recalls how to survive
by sucking in, gulping air
taking deep long breaths feverishly
trying to survive after being
in a chokehold for 8.5 minutes

Here the nation remembers:
Eric Garner, Briyonna Taylor, Ahmaud Arbery, George Floyd
Here the nation learns again how to   *breathe*
Freely!

Bless Us, Lord, for the Sin-Free Life We Are Living

I stare with my gaping mouth
mock and revere
at this whimsical reality
eyes rolling in disbelief
head bowed in silence
knees scraping at the pew
to absolve my sins.

We only bow down to the fear of the unknown
the fear of being punished
by an exalted God in Heaven
carved in our faith
surviving generations
through reams of yellow-tinged holy scriptures.

Surrounded by a million slithering tongues and roving eyes
flooded by the shining spotlight
waiting for it to become a trend
to become a sensation,
for the ignorant minds to be aware
of the writhing pain
it has to catch fire   *and burn.*

Leaving marks on our suppurating skin
seething with blisters in the pain of losing
a loved one,
a life,
a country,
an identity.

It takes a million to march and protest on the roads
the sun scratching their faces
burnt and scathed by the injustice
screaming in silence
gutted like a fish in the open streets

thick blood staining the curbside
of the lands, we boisterously own.

The nakedness of humanity
staring through the gaping hole in his chest
shot in broad daylight
in the middle of the goddamn market.

We turn our eyes in shame
move our heads in disbelief
and thank our Gods in Heaven
to spare our loved ones
the ones we love,
the ones we care.

We move with our twisted spines
towards the house of Gods,
to worship the one sitting in Heaven
to suck away all our pain
and bless us with the sin-free life
we desire, a life in vain.

Does Hurt Have a Gender?

What does a body want when it breaks down into
a million pieces? Its pulverized existence wanting acceptance.

Only to be ignored and walked over. Leftover like day-old milk
on the kitchen counter. Forgotten and left to curdle.

Why do we keep numbing the sharp pain,
the knotted lamentation, caught in our hungry mouths?

That cuts our souls both ways and leaves us to bleed in this world.
Profused with sweat and blood. A moment, indescribable.

Leaking and soaking the ridges of the curbside;
Here the thickness of your blood, its viscosity

And the gravitas of your speech depends on the color of your skin.
A pain, untenable.

An insurmountable pain rising in my mouth.
A dichotomy between pain and acceptance. A desire, abominable.

Do screams have a religion too? Do cries have a race?
Does hurt have a gender? Do wounds have a nationality?

Does your tongue curl into sin when you call out my name?
Does the triteness of ideologies still mollify your pain?

Dead Constellation

Inspired by the low flying helicopters in NYC during the Black Lives Matter Protest

The electrified hum of fireflies has been maimed by the rumbling noise of choppers hovering in the dark skies of my city forming a fallacy of protection. Governed by the bright blinding lights, this city that never sleeps. *This city now weeps. This city now wails.* Suffocated and slaughtered to its core. The vast heaving bosom once adorned with the beautiful celestial bodies and constellations that once gave my nine-year-old son a reason to stay up late during the weekend. Tracing the skin of the cerulean skies with his supple fingers. Every star dazzling in his face. A streak of happiness ran across his face, stringing his hopes into a bright smile. Now all his nights have been roiled over by numbing strobing lights. *This city weeps. This city wails.* The lullaby at night has now been replaced by the rattling of black bones now forming the catacombs of the dead and forgotten. A frail skeleton of this dying city. A skeleton pitted with greed and violence sticking to its thick ribs like greed. A ghastly presence. A threatening acknowledgment of the presence of an anarchist, who rules with an iron fist. A mendacious President. The sidewalks have been pitted with bones of the dead which will rattle for generations haunting your lullabies. A strange camaraderie is lacing the wails of the widows that will rise through the dark alleys amidst the marred streets, which once looking up gave you the sense of direction, now leaves you lost like a broken compass. Clueless with tears streaming from the eyes of every black mother making the path similar to a protest outside my window. A cornrow of failed desires and rotten dreams. Now, I look outside the window of my high rise with the shimmering lights of the *Empire State* throbbing like a pulsating vein exhausted with a heaving sigh. As it counts yet another dawn in the city, whose skies are now arrested with the rumbling sounds of helicopters, forming a dead constellation.

Pain Like a Stray Dog Keeps Coming Back

I curl like a decaying fetus
dying under its muted stench
still & unmoving yet a remnant of creation.

Every curve of my body morphs and mold
carving a new letter of pain
within the folds of my skin.

Pain has its own language.
it moves in unknown ways
to emboss a new script, a dying language.

Pain, as it travels on my undulating spine,
holds my broken pieces together
like a prayer holding my soul.

I have cut myself to God in more ways than I can count
gluing the tattered pieces together
frayed ends, seams bursting apart.

Now it seems an empty task like the blackening elbows
of a widow on the window sill.
The inveterate hunger never finds its home.

Pain like a stray dog comes back to my doorstep
every morning begging its share,
Sorrow like a bag of heavy stones sits deep and heavy.

Every desire of mine holds a lien to my cracked pieces.
My hunger is nothing more than
an elegy of misplaced hope.

All Men are Created Equal

A black fleshy mouth like an open wound
gaping blindly in the thicket of the night with its jagged teeth

ready to devour with the slightest provocation
you hear a name said aloud ringing in your ears

bouncing off like fog from concrete, vague but familiar
you are running toward an illusion, a silhouette of your dreams

being woven for generations and yet the threads are fraying apart
bursting at the seams, unable to hold the cries of black mothers and sisters

a whole generation of wailing widows goes unheard, running stark naked in the streets
carrying a bowlful of questions in their palms, laced with the blood of their firstborns

who doused in that maternal blood to become the ebony dreams
still twinkling in the weary cracked smiles of their mothers

and sisters, wives, and countless unnamed faces running, running, running-
who were close to seeing life in its nubile beauty just before it is

snatched away into the darkness, by the sudden jolt of a body as
it takes the bitter strength of a bullet lodged between its ribs

a gaping hole, a dark black hole showing the nakedness of this nation
that reports another shooting of a black body

lying unclaimed, lynched to death in this country built on the
phantom claims of life, liberty, and pursuit of happiness.

An Act of Self Defense

After Ahmaud Arbery

The exact moment when the grief takes
shelter in your heart leaving you undone
when the emptiness sits in a gaping hole
an abyss of loneliness

the deafening lull in your mind
stops making sense
Your ears ring with
the lonely wail of the widow
in the apartment above you

Sorrow takes a different shape
tears streaming down incessantly
for the senseless acts of violence and cowardice
carried out by the very educated hands of this land
where life, liberty, and pursuit of happiness are
foundations of society, the sidewalks of those
pitted with the black bones of their own

You are not carrying your freedom in your hands
/your right to bear arms/
when the only right you give to a mother
is to stick a cross in the middle of an unknown street
giving a piece of land for her dead son
a parched island of grief:

There is nothing but death at the end of a gun.

When the names keep adding to the unnamed list
Treyvon, Michael, Eric,...and so on
an ever-growing list of dead and forgotten
where names have to scream out loud
to make their lives matter else all hell will break loose

To hell with your right to the *Second Amendment*
when it is laced with the blood
of a black brother,
whose murder you are incessantly
trying to justify as self-defense.

Transformation

"They buried us, but they didn't know we were seeds."
— Dinos Christianopoulos, A Greek Poet

You tried to ruin me but after being tormented for eons,
mutilated and spliced walking barefoot on the shards

of my pulverized dreams. I have risen like a phoenix
from the ashes to smear the faces of those

who mocked, tormented me, and numbed my voice
for speaking the truth, ringing loud and clear

around the patriarchal naysayer's, those who believe,
that pain and angst can be molded and morphed for their own benefit.

Those who believe that money can be churned out from those
whose wails and screams are lacing your blood-washed streets

You tried to ruin, bury me in the depths of ignorance and abuse,
Forgetting I will rise like molten lava from the womb of Gaia

and erase your existence in a blink of an eye.
You tried to ruin me but you turned me into a warrior,

A blind seed ready to branch out.

Blood on Our Hands

Walking on the waterfront next to my high-rise condo thoughts and epiphanies rush like a mixed stream of water carrying the dust and the silt. The thought of knowing that nothing touches us more deeply than the thought of dying alone. Strange things have happened in the past few months and the earth continues to burn and enrage and express its wrath against us. We, the puny creation, in this universe, cannot save us, anymore. I'm sitting down near the water, gazing at the cerulean skies and waiting for all this to come down, and like a Tsunami to wipe the slate clean. The pause in our lives intermixed with the hullabaloo and chaos within our hearts could not be tamed as *Nietzsche* once said. "*It could not birth a dancing star. Not Always.*" We human beings are worshippers of destruction and mayhem. Everything we engulf and masticate like a fleshy peach only to spit out the dried seeds for the generations to follow. Burning cedars and the blazing redwoods are a witness to these atrocities. The crimson-tinged skies suffocated and fogged by the thickness of our hunger and the incessant greed carried by men for generations. This flagellation of unbearable bounds has seeped into our lives and like a night with its black teeth is devouring our insides. This contagion declaring its boisterous presence in a span of hundred years tells us, this is the moment of pause and silence. This is the moment where you stop and notice the blood on your hands and the flesh between your teeth.

Asphyxiated

Inspired by the death of Gambian British photographer Khadija Mohammadou Saye who was killed in the Grenfell Tower Fire in 2017. The survivors of Grenfell are still awaiting justice, while the official inquiry refuses to recognize the systemic racism of social inequality and institutional response as contributing to the disaster.

They say *"Eyes are the window to the soul"*
yet yours are shuttered tight,
saturated with injustice and discrimination
birthing around you in every passing moment
the raging flames engulfing the last sliver
of hope;
of light,
of love
sucking out from every single soul
holding onto their dear loved ones
in that fateful tower that day.

They say, *"An artist takes in the beauty
through their eyes"*
and yet yours are closed
overwhelmed with the injustice
the raging inequality;
hoping for the day, the perfect utopia,
where everyone is blessed with the
basic privilege
to live;
to love,
to breathe.

They say, *"Eyes are the embodiments
of the soul"*
a metaphor for the muted language;
spoken between the souls
and yet yours are closed shut
averting the view from
all the hunger and greed

burning & leaving
the stench of devouring flames
a putrid stench of indifference
towards your life

They say, *"Take in the world through all your senses"*
and yet you devoid yourself
from this ethereal experience
as your world burns down from inside
screaming and whelping,
the injustice leaves welts and blisters
on your suppurating skin

When the empty words shower like
the scarring acid rain
on your open wounds
you scream,
you wail in the hollow nights
hoping for a single soul
to lend their ear
to hear you,
hear you screaming
I can't breathe!!!

Demarcation

A reflection on the broken prison system of the United States of America.

That frail evening marking
the shadows of the long summer days
a bird perched on the barbed wires of the prison
demarcating happiness and the grief
acceptance and rejection,
solitude and the bouts of laughter,
the prisoner and the free

the arresting height of that boisterous wall
whose bricks are soaked
with the crackling wails and sobs
of the broken souls
neatly carved and plastered

a bizarre tinge of the ochre
peeling off from the walls
as the tears flow incessantly
through bleary eyes as
they gaze from emptiness to nothing
silence culled in hollow bones
rattling with rage

palms holding out
for someone, something
for forgiveness,
a fleeting touch of humanity
a soft supple touch of love

a day wrapped around
the promises of second chances
silhouette of the loved ones
appearing between the thick bars
a pleasant sight for the cracked and pale eyes
death and silence are interchangeable

Go ask the bird
as it sits at the barbed wire fence
keeping the two realms separate
a socially justifiable demarcation
between the cacophony and the melody
the symmetry and the dissonance
between the pristine and the ostracized

How thin is the separation between
love and acceptance?
despair and the second chances,
between judged and forgiven.

The People We Love, the People We Care

In these profound moments of history where the pause and activism have become inextricably tangled between these moments of isolation, is the incessant desire to be heard and touched. Hunkered down with our version of reality, we all are hoping fervently to add our voices to the global language of grief. This language is ringing off the concrete like the smell of fresh blood of the black body lacing the sidewalks of this nation. This chaotic fumigation of this potent moment has been engraved daily in the hearts and minds of the people, whose tongues have been lolling for generations. Unable to decipher the pain and toxicity of the language, this system has been oiled with. This system's suppression and aggregation take the shape of a chokehold and leave a thick impression on the black necks around the nation where the protectors devour. Laced with their anger, thick as greed, and laughing boisterously in the naked streets of this nation. The nation which weeps. The nation which now wails. This ineradicable beauty is precisely what we must fight so hard to defend. This galvanizing call has now become the international flashpoint that should be reflected to those holding the reins to power, the reins to history, the reins to this moment. They should remind themselves again and again that this collective grief pouring from the sidewalks, streets, parking lots, and crowded lanes is a callout for the people we love, the people we care.

A Revolution By Choice

Much has changed during the last few months. Life has been changing and being stagnant at the same time. I stand here at the intersection of this moment bearing witness to the shifting gaze of time, through the lens of people, through the story of the dead and the forgotten. Much has yet to be spoken and yet to be heard as we swiftly move away from the beginning of the year. As we move through the crossroads of this surreal moment, a bookmark in the history of moments, where we stand six feet apart yet appear as a witness to this crowdsourced event. The moment that holds the dichotomy of past and present and stays juxtaposed in this surreal hiccup of time. Where we realize our feet are touching this scorched earth, laced with human atrocities for eons, as our eyes watch this revolution unfurling in the streets. Where the fearless *Athenas* are appearing, speaking power to the truth, brushing shoulders in the protest-laced streets, where we know we can survive if we have enough compassion and empathy to let others survive. Where the collective grief and voices screaming and gasping for breath in a chokehold for 9.29 minutes has now become a war cry for the revolution. Where white silence is counted as abuse. Where privilege is not defined by the color of your skin. Where the man stands witness to his own sins. Where the god's hands are no longer creating a perfect creature but a man of imperfections. When we can see our reflection in the mirror and say to ourselves, *this is the moment that belongs to me*, a change, a revolution that I birth by choice.

II. War and Peace

In the First Week of the New Decade, Humanity Stands Singed

After the political tension between Iran and the United States in the first week of 2020

Not a week has gone by and I smell the blistering taste
of my dreams, my desires,
my mornings,
my hopes,
as an aftertaste
the unending hunger of humankind
at the back of my throat

this revenge of monstrous proportions
this boisterous rage,
this chest-thumping attitude
has been a curse
if only God could tell,
break his silence for once
for the benefit of all kind

On the verge to obliterate
each and every small hope
desires and wishes birthing in the palm of a child
hope resting carelessly
on the end of a curved smile
waiting on the fallen eyelashes
ready to make a wish sublime

This inveterate hunger can't be doused
by a territorial declaration
where boundaries are nothing
but a limitation of mankind
to share anything which is
pure and true

Like Nature,
Like the monsoon dance of the peacocks,

Like the wings of a monarch,
Like a symphony,
Like a serenade,
Like all good things lost and forgotten

These lines reek of blood,
war, death, starvation, and loneliness
these lines are not marking our possessions
these lines are
cutting,
piercing,
slicing our dreams into halves
bleeding on both ends unbidden

Here at the start of the decade,
humanity stands parched
humanity stands singed.

A Fistful of Grain

After the genocide in Bosnia, Sudan, Iraq, Rwanda, Syria

As the rumbling bulldozers move through her town
the earth-shattering truth starts
taking place in the hearts
of her people all around

Clinging to the lost faith of her fading grace
She waited for someone, *anyone*
to save her from being skinned alive
dumped in pieces

When faith becomes your biggest enemy
targeted for praying to the Gods not known to many,
you will be kicked around and gutted
stripped of your dignity

Monsters hungry for power
chest thumping their existence,
take away the last sliver of hope
from her bleared eyes seeding them with pain

Sorted and arranged
like pieces of meat on a slab,
She will be devoured
slowly and feverishly
till her ashen soul cannot last

A displaced identity and a make-believe home
is her safe haven now,
her eyes dream of nightmares
bringing alive every night of that slaughterhouse

Those mighty bulldozers--
that once built her beautiful city

gleaming with minarets and lush lanes,
are now used to dig mass graves
for her only son, peacefully buried,
with a fistful of grain.

Missed Boat

My home burnt down to ashes
walls painted with new shades of gore
a new shade of limestone and grey:
with fingers dipped in the blood
of my beautiful loved souls

My streets are laced
with death and macabre
the wailing cries of widows,
his lost son--with his broken bike
eating dust evermore

With dried-up trails on the face
eyes gazing from emptiness to nothing,
has painted a picture
of a new broken being

I'm digging hopelessly
with my bloody knuckles
looking for lost hope
in the pile of death and fear
trying to cover my back
with the last piece of
borrowed bread and tattered cloth

I'm trying to keep myself alive
knowing all the faces I have known
have been fed to the bloodhounds
in all its glory

I couldn't care less about
the orphaned kid next door
whose birth I celebrated
and danced for till my feet went sore

All I care about now,
is that I should run and hide
like hunted prey,
make sure not to miss the boat
which will take me
to the promised lands
far far away.

Living in a War Zone

Where have all the flowers gone to die?
Why does the sun never rise
and death and misery
have become part of life?

Small hands clasp the dead
the lanes and the gully
are marked by cadavers
death constantly piling.

Screams are gut-wrenching and numbing
the soul is burdened
under the burden of carrying the weight of death
and is slowly crumbling.

He stands alone cold and dry,
tears streaming from his haggard face
and he has a question
everyone should face.

Why the street he ran to his heart's content,
to fly his beautiful kite
and dusty place he hid
to play the game of hide and seek,
are all muddied with blood and disgrace?

Where are giggles and laughs hiding?
A place he once called his *home,*
now stands a charred broken place
barely alive.

Why are the hopes and dreams
crouched and suffocated in the deep thick smoke?
Where did they hide all the broken toys
he once adored?

He stands there confused and broken-hearted
in a country where love and humanity
have parted ways and left him to rot
alone in their place.

Why is this land once brimming with
luxury and grace
now defeated and defaced?

Why have all the places
he could run and play
become pitted with makeshift mass graves?

Tourniquet: Snapshot of a War-Torn House

a patch of green growing
in the living room of a war-torn house
leaves growing out of the cracks
the door unhinged now lying asunder

ceiling shredded into a thousand elegies
to the blue sky, a lone witness
to the massacred shreds torn thin
as the promise of life

muted and dumbfounded
sometimes it needs more
than a lone promise of God
in a home to heal

sharpened with deafening silence
sorrow morphs and molds in its own ways
death has its own language
a razor-sharp vernacular:
a wailing widow in the streets

A half-broken frame of the window
once laced with laughter
seeping into the cracked tiles
of this house with sepia-tinged walls
memories peeling off like
a broken promise left
on the kitchen-shelf to curdle

a tiny green patch growing
through this broken house
healing with every sapling--
every tiny leaf growing
through the cracks
breaking through the pain.

What Can Be the Purpose of Prayer?

What else can be the purpose of prayer? Kneeling at the pew;
the line of the concrete etching in your soft knees.
Sometimes redemption feels like self-flagellation.

Tears don't represent my repentance anymore.

This dichotomy of emotions has fooled humanity for eons.
Even the crocodile's eyes tear up while devouring the prey.
What else are we celebrating secretly,
with those salty globules running down our cheeks?
Who knows?

Deception is our facade for survival.

My fake smiles of empathy and compassion,
reek through the tattered face of the
homeless whom I pass by every morning.
I need to fix my route for running. My self-defined priority.

The disparity between the theory and praxis is inevitable.

My needs and wants are not pivoted or angled anymore.
They circumvent my ego and self-boasting.
We brag about winning like my cat for every mouse she hunts.

Pulls out of her teeth. Splayed on my white marble. Never to eat. Blood staining the floor.
Entrails as a proud achievement. Her teeth grinning as a measure of self-assurance.

What else can be the purpose of prayer?

Me with my naked self arranging my desires neatly in front of God
keeping a safe distance between the wants and needs.
looking for affirmation evermore.

III. My Body Is Not An Apology

Even My Grief Should Be Productive

Don't let the aroma leave the pickle jar.
Keep the lid tight
my granny used to say.
Some things are better left unspoken.
Part of your tradition—
scream but not too loud.
Let the grief resonate within the inside of your skin.

We are picked and chosen precariously
through callous thick fingers
Make sure they are not rotten...not stained enough
the flavor doesn't come through well.
I choose my memories
precariously - not the rotten ones
the shuddering truth:
It should not shatter the patriarchy.

Let the anger morph.
Let it churn into the vermilion shade
the symbol of pride and ownership:
Use your pain wisely,
let them own you well.

I used those broken whispers as a guide
to pluck the radishes out from the broken mud
of the vegetable garden
moistened and broken by the summer rains,
crumbled in pieces
but always rich in bounty.

With bended knee scraping my soft skin.
I lowered myself whitened
by the heat of the summer sun
sweat and tears inseparable. A perfect concoction of pain.

A wicker basket filled to the brim
by the end of the day with the fruit of my labor
grief pulled out from the dearth of acceptance.
A menagerie of suffocated desires
laid bare for your eyes.

A lesson I have learned through the years
that even my grief should be productive.

False Ownership

This is strangely annoying,
when you see arrogance in
someone who doesn't own a thing
can't conjure a thing out of thin air
let alone a human being.

You are just the renter here. You don't own shit.
you are born from this womb
that cradles your existence for months
a sliver away from called a being.

Nothing but a pulsating existence in a foreign body
Sometimes the body treats it like an infection
to keep away the contamination
self-purging, an act of reclamation.

Sometimes it accepts
cups its own palm
supports you, carries it to term.
Its the body
the arrangement,
the unsaid understanding
a solemn promise;
between the body and its identity.

Your existence is slowly molded
like a ball of sagging clay on the potter wheel
morphed and molded
to be called a human being.

You don't own the womb.
You definitely don't own our bodies.
You break the arrangement
just like to possess the things.

Let me clear this,
for the sake of your understanding
the body is not for your taking.
There is a thin line between
The choices we make and your wanting.

Entry/Exit

Pain unable to hide between its own shadows, where grief goes to hide.
Shuddering ripples cleaving the body in half like a painful carving.

Shreds of pain hiding like crumbs between the covers. Language chiseled like
the hunters' knife on the naked skin of the wild oak donning a false sense of ownership.

Your breath on my skin spits and marks its boundaries. Your words carve out
the burnished wounds. The bourgeois display of pain splayed for the whole world.

To whom does this body belong? Suffering is nameless. Carved out of the tongues of those
who abused us. Misunderstood and mispronounced like a foreign language.

A penny tightly clutched in the soft palm leaves impressions.
An uprooted oak falls silently in the naked woods.

A lot has entered and exited through this body leaving behind the remnant of painful
memories carving their names. A litany of wild acclaim.

My scorched skin covered with suppurating welts and blisters.
Skin begging for sustenance. Sometimes, even scorched earth goes green.

I wait patiently for the rain to come. Earth trowled over and remains fertile.
Nature teaches me resilience. The parched body craves the sustenance of the monsoon rains.

Sometimes a body forgets its own memories, living and breathing through the pain.
Forgetting its own entry and exit. Succumbed to life living trapped shut.

Mouth

Our mouth is an entry point. It speaks of hunger,
speaks of lust. The urgency of something more sacred
than the hymns under muted breath.

It speaks of the violence bodies endure.
A gaping wound for our broken soul.
An unspoken lexicon of silence
but misheard and misunderstood.

Desires birth within it.
Anything that catches our attention
needs to be validated by our mouths.
the epicenter of gluttony—
the protagonist of the original sin.

The desirous taste should sit well
before we can call it our own.
We call a lot of things our own.
We desire.
We possess.
The most untamed of all senses.

A shiny trinket catches our attention
and the slurping desire starts building.

We are creatures of the mouth.
We are creatures of wanting.

My Body Is Nothing but a Sack of Blades

Pain moving like a fracture, opening the crevasse.
A gaping wound. An entry into the blind cave of my numb memories.

The putrid smell of the burnished wounds scraped for time eternal
The wound loses the tourniquet to sullen time. Cuts and deepens.

Drips. Like blood in the water. Drips and stains. *Again.*

Anointing everything it touches. An outward growing fractal of pain.
Growing and overshadowing.

Night devouring everything with its black teeth. Tongue lolling,
slithering with desire. Sometimes touching a wound marks its existence.

My body is nothing but a sack of blades. An elegy for misplaced hope.

An open mouth of a blind well, where time loses its existence.
A dull blade. Every insult sharpening the edge a bit more.

The Day the Town Celebrated

A response to honor-based killings around the world

A stone thrown in a silent lake breaks its skin. Pain travels like ripples.
An outward fractal of grief continuously growing with every passing moment.

A single shot piercing through their soft bodies.
Piecing them with hate stringing the town.

Truth gaping through the open wound.
A lone gunfire shredding the sky into a million screams.

Only in this version love was not ostracized—
but burned and hanged in the town square.

Hanged like pieces of meat for the devouring eyes circling them.
A prized possession for the caste that rules with an iron fist.

A mother runs half-naked through the empty street. *Wailing.*
Anger fracturing the thatched roofs.

Pain scratches like a pellicle dissolving in acid.
Its stench carried for generations.

Like folklore passed on from one babbling tongue to another.
How the little town's gazed gaping mouth like a blind cave

The time when love was not ostracized. Caste and creed were thrown aside
when that small town gathered to celebrate the honor killing.

Unappreciated

How can you live a life when the moments are
as long as the shrug of your shoulder?
Or waiting on the careless fingers resting on a trigger
marked and unappreciated

How can you live a life
when you are judged by your
cast/creed/skin color?
Or how your tongue moves inside you when you speak of love?
Those scriptures the world has forgotten
while your knees are scraped blue
kneeling for praying to gods in Heaven

How can you live a life
when your desire and the rage of hormones
or sex resting between your supple thighs,
marks and etches you?
and you can only exist in binary form
any other is a direct violation of the life
soon to be dissolved,
should cease to exist

How can you live a life
like a broken spine of a book?
Still holding rotten pages together
the essence soaked in between tattered pages
but too old to be lifted off the shelves
thrown and resting on a frail broken armchair

How can you live life like this?
Tell me, can you?

resistance

I don't wait for you to corroborate my truth
evidence to prove the finality of my desires

I don't wait for your soft touches to smooth my scars
a tourniquet to stop this bleeding

I don't want you to comfort me in the middle of the night
only to unravel my pain in the morning

as my body goes from a shade darker than yesterday
I don't need the assurance of the revolution around the corner

I birth my own revolution
and I create my own marches
the truth my soul owes to nobody but me

a conversation with my higher self
a divine ablution.
When I resist
I create.

Freedom, an interpretation

What does freedom mean to me, a dandelion?
as I continue my tryst
with the boastful wind
as it carries my identity
on its fleeting wings

I tried with all my might
to hold onto my identity
but the cruel and the mighty winds
uprooted and carried me

I'm carried by my need
and desire to be rooted again
I'm an immigrant in my own
godforsaken land

I reach with all my failing might
with my bits severed
falling and rooting
clutching to the ground for its sustenance

See, I have to survive
this atrocity called war
/supposed peaceful settlement/
and rise through it
find a new patch of soil
to call itself my home

dig my roots deeper to survive
the cold transformation
of the ever-changing world
I now own

these boundaries and lines
don't make sense to me

when my identity has been
dragged and redefined
I end up getting branded as an
Immigrant.

Hashtag Games

We play hashtag games
every time the evil scratches its belly
hunger plays on its forked tongue
mocking humanity.

A tag for every survivor
a label for everyday
smears the face with its ashen truth
justice delayed is justice denied
they willfully say.

A day to mourn the loss
where some girl regrets life
her dreams broken and pulverized
dying a muted death
the day changes
atrocity switches masks
a new hashtag and pain take a new shape.

A New March,
a new route to follow
new placards to paint
new colors to wallow.

We keep strangulating our moments
life being squeezed out of them
Black Mondays and Dark Fridays
the debilitating pain;
till we find the new low and start all over again.

We play hashtag games
victims change faces
a hamster on a wheel:
but the perpetrator
remains the same.

My Body Is Not an Apology

This body–
My body is not an apology
It's a prayer.
Forgiveness wrapped in the filigrees end of my skin
frayed at the ends;
battered for so long
by your pointy convictions
and cookie-cutter rules that try
to shape and mold this body along.

My body is not an apology.
It doesn't desire to fit in a frame
mapped inch by inch
else to be ashamed.

My body is not an apology.
It's a roar:
a declaration
an unapologetic, unabashed
straight in-your-face truth
a war cry:
a deafening scream from the silence.

My body is not an apology
This body will not be mapped
as a benchmark for beauty,
an attempt to hide crows-feet
or the spider veins,
from your vile eyes
and your forked tongue.

My body is not an apology
But a safe haven
an epitome of affection,
a metaphor for crimson love
that flows in my veins for years to come.

My body is not an apology
It's an eye of the storm
A dance of destruction,
A safe haven for life
forgiveness in disguise.

With love neatly folded in the wrinkles of my skin
warmth oozing from every pore of my being
a lesson etched in every single crow's feet
forgiveness written through every inch of me.

This body is not an apology.
It is a profound lesson
a triumphant proclamation;
an unfettered declaration.

IV. A Just Immigration Policy

Unforgivable

After U.S. Border Agents destroyed supplies left for migrants

The rugged terrain of those unforgiving lanes
the ones warmed by the scorched feet
parched throats,
these blisters and welts have a story to tell
suppurating skin begets mercy.

Dreams glimmering in those bleary eyes
shimmering with the hopes of a foreign land
across the barbed wires,
whose pointy edges deemed softer
than the poking end of an AK 47 rifle on my naked throat.

Dreams shattered
my brown land turned into a deviant ocher shade
that rust,
the blood infested infection
devoured my childhood
slowly sucking away the sliver of air from my chest
a contagion unknown.

My heart is pounding in my chest.
ghosts of past resonating in the folds of my skin
the heart that still keeps the land of love neatly folded
like a pressed *Dahlia*. The faint strains of its fragrance
still, lace my dreams at night.

Every turn and twist in the path
takes us nearer to the hope of finding a solace
in the land foreign to me.

Like a fly trapped in the window frame
feverishly-
I'm fleeing towards the lands of my salvation

Eyes bulging out, skin whitened by the summer sun
frail limbs, scorched back.

You can carve the silhouette of my bony frame
in your milky moonlight
I carry the prayers for your unborn child
prayers taught by grandmother
in my pursed lips, a sacred hymn.

You are the savior of my pulverized hopes
a sliver of a hope slowly withering,
but the dreams turn into a nightmare
seeing the air whizzing out of my newborn
a curse for a mother—
heaving chest burying the stench of death.

How can you save the soul of a country?

A symbol of life, liberty, and pursuit of happiness
a country made from the colorful skin of millions
when you throw away the water: Our *sustenance*
empties it on a dusty trail
in defiance of the love you once held.

The Day Liberty Was Disrobed

The serrated voices of mottled fear
in those syllables
the smattering cacophony,
the syntax and semantics of unspoken fear
as if everything makes sense around you
except for you,
except for the voices in your head.

We plead to them to hear us once
just once,
before they carve out the pointy convictions
and chisel them to suit their needs
mold them back into the cookie-cutter mold
caulked by the hands of this unforgiving world.

Carving out the words from your tongue
that is free and unabashed,
You hold nothing more than a muted opinion
falling on deaf ears standing on the curbside
stained by the blood of the unspoken and the untold.

The collective conscious
living and breathing for generations
has lost their sanity
staying on the rim of the edge
of darkness and grim,
like the limestone shade of death.

How do you speak?
How do you voice your opinion anymore?

When the epitome of life, liberty, and pursuit of happiness
the one which stands by the *Golden Door*
has been scratched and engraved
a playground for graffiti carved by immoral hands.

To satiate the unending hunger of Cerberus
those who hold the leash to freedom,
are now guarding our speech and thoughts
redefining the solemn words written for centuries.

Those with their slithering tongues
and taloned fingers
are scraping and scratching
the last bits of life
from our solemn statue
our epitome of liberty.

True Lies

This lack of emergency
this hunger frothing between our teeth
we cuss and words are shredded between our teeth
there can never be the truth
so pure and lies, so vile
that cannot be told these days

our ears are burned at the tips
truth is acidic some days
with eyes peeled in amazement
for the vileness flooding the streets
and filling up newspapers

those lies screaming
at the top of their tongues
and hounding at
the right of the dial
those incessant pictures
running on the reels
like a hamster on the wheel

we gulp down
this atrocious fake truth
and true lies
every damn day
and every single night

Conjecture

What lilies are blooming outside the four walls of my room with no name?

The seasons pass without waving goodbye—
there are only so many things I chose to ignore this year

Hunkered inside my room, I am counting hollow shadows crossing the streets
tender sapling breaking open through the moist crumbled earth

Douse with the monsoon rains. Empty seasons pass outside these walls
like the phantom shadows beside a moving train, a fallacy of time passing.

Days rolled into nights like incessant numbers on my calendar.
A hamster on a wheel life with memories etched on our dead and the dying

Counting the loss by every passing day, *I wonder* what lilies are blooming in
the square today? Loneliness begets acceptance, bodies shriveled like raisins
craving warm acceptance.

What buds have birthed in the small garden, *I wonder*.
Some losses are too heavy to count, some debts are too big to pay.

All my passing seasons are now a conjecture of my empty mind
Trapped inside the sepia-tinged walls of my high rise, burgeoned by the grief

Like a father blackening his elbows on the window sill
counting his breaths like long scratches on a prison wall.

I Don't Need a Messiah

Like the grains seeping through the palm
you cannot stop pain sweat and tears
I will storm through
the other side of your wall
paving my way as I move;
I don't need a messiah,
I don't need another you.

The boundary, the fine lines
which separate us all
like the blood gnashed
between clenched teeth,
I will seep my way through
I don't need a messiah,
I don't need another you.

Young innocent blood staining the curbside
washed on the streets
where precious freedom
is gutted like a fish;
filling the dirt pools
their gaping mouths carrying
the nakedness of the nation
for the bleary eyes to see
I don't need a messiah,
I don't need another you.

I will wade in the strongest of the tide
you shifty-eyed moon
you can turn the waves
all you want,
I will break the chains myself
I don't need a messiah,
I don't need another you.

We Never Protest, We Never Do

Watch how the silence convulses
and balances itself precariously
tiptoeing on the fleeting moments of this time
this time:
this merciless time
has left everyone here
bereft of the emotion

like a stranger in a country
where you stand like a post without a flag
how these emotions deceive us
where we are craving
for the birth of these seraphic verses

Yes, language was used by the divine
before it got stained between our yellow teeth
laced with lies and deception
What good has it bought for
generations to generations?

when the need arrives and the same
words hurt like knives
a square knob inside a circular opening
lodged and scraping the ends of my throat
but we never spat out the truth
Oh! we never do

we watch as mute spectators
loneliness etched in the black of your eyes
like the bleary eyes of an orphan,
and we never protest, yes we never do
we hold onto our precious words
like bundles of old currency in a foreign country.

Are You Listening, World?

I'm nowhere close to being a ball of anxiety
spooling continually in the close corridors of life
unraveling pain which has always been a secret task
a hushed affair:

The unbroken trails of tears have yet again
dusted by the ashes of dead and unknown
screaming from the headlines of the paper,
lying helpless at our doorsteps
waiting to be hauled in
we are averting our eyes to living these days

waiting for them to disappear in the dark cleavage of the night
that ashen night;
a witness of thousand incessant cries
a mother's wail is loudest than any noise you ever heard
Are you listening, World?
Are you listening, still?

When her womb has been scrubbed and scratched
with her hands tied behind her back
when her heaving bosom has become
pools of salty tears
I scratch my pain
and see growing in my scrawny veins
like the spider web--they are reaching everywhere.

This uncontrolled growth of sadness,
an ever-expanding pattern of grief,
does it satiate your hunger for freedom
when you lay lien to their souls
abandoned on the other side of the barb wires
their skin bearing the scratches of inhumanity?

I wake every day taking a deep breath
inhaling the air laced with the tears of five years olds
stripped away from love
an unmapped land carved around the gilded cage
their new home,
and exhaling my share of freedom
in a land built on the pursuit of life liberty and happiness.

Requiem for a Dream

The one-horned night pokes cleaves you in half
& coagulates all your experience into a thick slimy liquid

Dripping through all parts of your porous soul when
the imaginary has broken the leash and is now running stark naked,

Uncontrolled, unfettered, in the surreal fields lit
by the burnished sun birthing thousand moons

In your half-open eyelids as a requiem for a half-dream.
Suffused with deep sleep, with bated breath, gasping for air &

Resting on the soft ends of your fingertips like a fleeting touch
of a black and orange gilded Monarch, your hands stretched out,

Fingers clawed scooping away your share of lightness from the sky
laced with dying light of the day that sliver of happiness,

Throbbing like a heavy vein in your temple, hard,
heart racing, and fluttering, ears buzzing with the electrified

Hum of the fireflies dancing in the night. These naked moments of the
night cleaves your heart open, slices off in halves,

Leaves you standing under the ashen nights like a *Saguaro*
beckoning the dark skies. You finally become witness to this

Monstrosity of nature as it rattles you and wakes you
from your night with its black teeth.

Transgressions

Scooping the darkness from the break of dawn
the world sleeps sheepishly.

My eyes touch the inside of my half-open eyelids
as the soft light tries to mold my barbed desires.

There is always hunger and grief culled in these bones
where greed sticks to it like fat. Thick and heavy with yearning.

Wants churning into a darker shade. The tongue lolling boisterously,
braving its existence between chiseled sharp teeth.

Black numbness of the night slowly petaling like the age-old wallpaper
in my sepia-tinged room. Coiling under the weight of its cravings,

the hunger cleaves my soul marking its territory, anointing
every inch of my existence.

I exist, cutting and living through the pain. Sharpening through every insult,
waiting for my transgressions to rear their ugly heads. Surreptitiously.

A Just Immigration Policy

Fear masquerading through
stone-cold heart and icy veins
diversity is a curse these days
a stain in the tapestry of humanity

we are trying to lighten the fabric
they say,
less browning more white
it looks better at night

the night when the moon turns ashen
crimson with the blood
running in sluice at the border walled-city
where laughter is lost
but at least the chickens are "cage-free"

a body rejecting its own blood
sweat and the slime mixed together
bellies sucked in
you can count their ribs
a silhouette of my skeleton frame,
in the frothy moonlight
of your free country

where the water pitchers
are satiating the thirst of
stones and the dirt trails
whitened by the summer sun
keeping the parched throats
still scratched and itchy

scarring the innards
of their marred skin
with their bony taloned fingers
trying to scrape

the stench of refugee camps
out of their yellow skins

There is a method to your inhumanity
a perfect excuse,
an unapologetic application of
your *just* immigration policy.

V. My Body Lives Like A Threat

Path to My Freedom

Walking precariously on the steep path
chosen by the boisterous men
tiptoeing between the serrated ends
of misogyny and inequality.

With a whimper and a roar
I walk,
I run,
when the ground beneath my feet morphs and tumbles,
when every war of mine
is nothing but a mere screech to this tone-deaf patriarchy.

I laugh at the incredulity of pain
a tightrope strung between the dreams and reality,
bowing down in obedience
walking with a stoop of discipline
with the freedom, you have handed me on the plate
like I was the chosen one, you see.

My head pointing towards cerulean skies
laced with dreams and equality,
the pain of unspoken truths for generations
still lodged in my throat
I challenge my resolution
the fear of losing seeded deeply.

But I never give up—
as I learned from the footsteps of warriors
the path to my freedom is laced
with the blood of my determination
which their shameful eyes still can't bear to see.

My Survival Story

The slow cleaving in my backbone
a seamless transformation:
branching into my thousand selves
like a sapling breaking
from the blind seed
I'm sprouting, I am thriving.

Growing like a Medusa
this fecundity of myself,
breaking out into
thousand versions of me
morphing into shapes
perfecting the art of topiary.

Like a reflection of the summer sun
shining into a million versions of me,
on shards of broken mirror
blessing them with its apricity.

I'm the war cry, the mortal fear
residing behind enemy lines
the lava, the primordial gel
creating life so sublime,
I'm the knowledge in the verse
in the smattering cacophony of your mind.

With inked breaths and walnut skin
boisterous, unfettered, and uncontrolled,
walking barefoot on this graveled path
unspooling life's fears in its intimate corridors.

My pain impaled on the stars in the nightly sky
I shine through my pulverized skin,
the broken pieces I foraged together

to make a whole of me
an untrammeled beauty within.

This fecundity is my survival instinct
to handle the plethora of emotions
life throws at me,
undulating between the proximity and prosody of pain:
I'm learning. Yes, I'm growing.

The Burden We Are Passing On

Love arises out of acceptance
in a land made of broken bones
which rattles and hums a
lullaby in the soft light of the moon

Dig deep in the dirt with your dirty ankles
you can find the souls buried
under your sidewalks
Standing knee-deep in the river of blood
leaving footprint everywhere you go
such is the legacy we are leaving behind

There is an absence of the melody
the wind reeking of the hunger
lone tune of the pied piper is ruling the day
trying to proselytize the truth

We are losing our kids to this damn sea, I say.
Not a light or sparkle in those ashen eyes
robbed of their dreams as the sparrows
lose shadows to the evening sun.

The darkness plays in its bounty and hunger prevails.
This town, left as a grieving metaphor
for the catacombs,
no longer holds life in its broken lap.

Fingers bloodied with the blood
of sacrificed newborns
the ones you have masticated the life from
bony shoulders carrying the burden
for generations to come.

Safekeeping

The question begins where everything ends. An unmarked destination.
Every hunger has a bowlful of answers ready to be gulped down

to satiate the lingering thirst stuck in our parched throats for eons.
Every gaze strikes with the pinpoint precision

of holding the ones responsible for bringing us to this state,
we are dwelling in. A shared state of collective grief.

We know where all this pain and hatred comes from.
Like a deluge swapping off mankind and like a strong turbulent

flow sweeping the nation under its flow. Where has all this ramped-up
anger and injustice been buried for generations?

Where were the entry points for the catacombs in this city,
hiding for so long chewing and spitting out its half-eaten narratives.

The flawed narratives. Where is the blind mouth of this cave that
devoured everything that was once black and beautiful?

How soft and supple were the arms of those who once
carried soft and tender love and passed it on

to the next generation like fingers laced with the aroma of bay leaves
infused with heritage. Those fingers, those ears, carrying the fabled voices of my ancestors.

Where was the deafening echo of voices now hushed and muted?
Which bottom of the dark well was the secret storage

for the bones of my ancestors, piling up to eternity? Now, we all hold in our palms
a bowlful of unpunctuated grief, living life like stragglers,

with grief jumping hoops as a generation. The question is not what needs to be done
with these pent-up emotions, but who do we give them to for safekeeping?

We All Rise Out of Love

My tongue twists and turns
trying to fit the cookie-cutter in a land unknown
the words put in my mouth
like the small portions— those *kaurs*
made by warm supple hands of my mother
gently waiting for the next one.

Her fingers always doused by the fragrance of bay leaves
turmeric tainted, the various shades
as she kneads the *atta*
and dispenses life lessons
in the kitchen on a warm summer day.

She taught me, kindness comes from the heart
but hunger pierces a man the most
so learn to soothe hunger
the lingering pain,
as she puts all her strength into kneading the *atta*
into a dollop of the milky moon.

My language is different than yours
I try fervently to explain to my son
who keeps correcting my pronunciation
as I teach him the basics of love
kindness and purity of heart.

Sometimes I wonder,
how this world
marred and demarcated by the boundaries
those twisted pronunciations,
would look beautifully kneaded together?

Like the lump of moon
sitting in the copper-clad *paraat* of my mother
waiting to rise out of warmth.

Legends:
kaur - morsels
paraat - a utensil to knead flour
atta - flour

My Body Lives Like a Threat

A wound opens its mouth
and becomes self-inflicting
just like the night
in its extreme—
vulnerable to a ray of light,
its existence challenged,
and yet it stands bravely,
unfettered by the challenges of the dawn.

As I catch the words in my mouth
my language becomes an open threat
my razor speech falling sharp
on your dull convictions
we always exposed, our deepest and softest parts to heal.
that's how the body learns
to heal,
to grow.

To be vulnerable is an elegy for acceptance.

We have hunger written all over us
with the ink as black as the mole
on your shoulder
challenging the frothiness of the moonlight.

My unspoken words sit like a welt
on my tongue in this foreign world
every time I twist my tongue
to shape a word,
I mispronounce your fear
a new threat is born.

Acknowledgments

I'm beyond grateful for the advice and support from my friends, family, and editor for bringing my debut full-length poetry collection to fruition. My eternal gratitude goes to all the advanced readers of my full length for believing in my work and encouraging me every step of the way. I'm humbled by the generosity of Dr. Thelma Reyna for writing the foreword. Immensely grateful to my editor, Edward Vidaurre, and all the folks at FlowerSong Press who made my dream come true. I'm deeply thankful to the artist Christy E. O'Connor for agreeing to use her sculpture entitled, "Carried Trauma" as the cover image that deeply resonates with the ethos of the poems in the book. Finally thankful to my son and husband for always believing in me and supporting me against all odds.

Thank you to these publications, in which these poems originally appeared or are forthcoming

First Place National Level Winner for Spring Robinson/ Red Mahogany Poetry Contest 2020
"Peace - A Metaphor For Denial"

As the World Burns, Indie Blu(e) Publishing:
"A Nation in Chokehold"
"In the first week of the new decade, humanity stands singed"

"Lift Your Voice", By Kissing Dynamite:
"Bless Us, Lord, For the Sin-Free Life we are Living"

Subterranean Blue Poetry:
"An Act of Self Defence"

War Cry against the Uterus, Wide Eyes publication:
"False ownership"

Praxis Magazine:
"Demarcation"

The Poet Anthology: War and Battle:
"Missed Boat"

Door is a Jar Magazine:
"Mouth"

Lumiere Review:
"Asphyxiated"

The Poet Magazine:
"Living in a War Zone"

Whisper and the Roar:
"My Body Is Not an Apology"

Mookychick:
"Even My Grief Should Be Productive"

The Rising Phoenix Review:
"Entry/Exit"

My Body Is Not an Apology, Finishing Line Press:
"My Body Is Nothing But a Sack of Blades"
"The Day the Town Celebrated"
"The Day Liberty was Disrobed"
"Are You Listening, World?"
"A Just Immigration Policy"
"My Body Lives Like a Threat"

Headline Poetry:
"resistance"

Moonstone Arts:
"True Lies"

Ofrendas Magazine:
"Hashtag Games"

Madness Muse Press:
"Freedom - An Interpretation"
"Unappreciated"

Writing for Peace, Dove Tales:
"Unforgivable"

National BEAT Poetry Foundation Anthology 2020:
"The Burden We Are Passing On"

SONKU Collective "Family Legacies" Spring 2020
"We All Rise Out of Love"

The Woman Inc "TWIBB Beyond Black Awards 2020 Finalist :
"Does Hurt Have a Gender?"

She Speaks Up, "Jessie Butler Poetry Anthology 2020 Finalist :
"Path To My Freedom"

First Place State Level Winner for NAMI Dara Axelrod Poetry Contest 2020
"My Survival Story"

About the Author

Megha Sood is a Pushcart-nominated Award-winning Poet, Editor, Author, and Literary Activist from Jersey City, New Jersey. She is an Associate Editor at journals *MookyChick*(UK), *Life and Legends* (USA), and a Partner in the Literary project *"Life in Quarantine" with* CESTA, Stanford University, USA. She is also a member of the *National League of American Pen Women(NLAPW)*, *Women's National Book Association*(WNBA), and advocacy member at *United Nations Association- US Chapter*.

Her 750+ works are featured in journals, magazines, newspapers including *Poetry Society of New York, PBS American Portrait, American Writers Review, Kissing Dynamite, Rising Phoenix Review*, and many more. Megha is a 2020 National Level Winner Spring Mahogany Lit Prize and a Three-Time State-level winner of the NJ Poetry Contest. Second Place winner in San Gabriel Valley Poetry Festival 2021, Shortlisted in Adelaide Literary Awards(2020), Poetry Super Highway (2020), Erbacce Prize(2020), TWIBB(2020), iWomanGlobalAwards(2020). She has also been Nominated *"Author of the Year"* by NY-based Spillwords Press.

She is also a Recipient of the 2021 Poet Fellowship from *MVICW(Martha's Vineyard Institute of Creative Writing)*. She recently received a "Certificate of Excellence" by Steven Fulop, Mayor, Jersey City, New Jersey. Her literary partnership *"Life in Quarantine"* with Stanford University has been presented in the *Open Education Global Forum 2020* and received mention in *Stanford Daily.* Her sonnet publication with *Poetry Society of New York* has been accepted as a *Summer Reading curriculum in University High School, Indiana, USA*. She also has been featured on the *PBS American Portrait.* Her works have also been in various US universities journals like Stanford University, University of Albany, Kent State University, Chicago University, and Arkansas University.

She has been chosen twice as the panelist for the Jersey City Theater Center Online Series *"Voices Around the World"* and *"The Box"*. Her works are selected numerous times by the Jersey City Arts Festival and the Department of Cultural Affairs. Her work inclines towards literary activism and generating awareness is the primary goal of her writing.

She is the Co-Editor of anthologies (*"The Medusa Project"*, Mookychick) and (*"The Kali Project,* Indie Blu(e) Publishing). "Tha Kali Project" has been a finalist in the *National Indie Excellence Book Awards 2021. She also is the author of* Chapbook (*"My Body is Not an Apology"*, Finishing Line Press, 2021) and Full Length (*"My Body Lives Like a Threat"*, FlowerSongPress, 2022). She has been a featured panelist on the *Women's National Book Association(WNBA-DC Chapter)* alongside Southern US Youth Poet Laureate, Alora Young.

Her Performing venues include the *New York Poetry Festival, Newark Arts Festival, Paterson Poetry Festival, Nuyorican Cafe, Hudson County Community College,* and many more. She blogs at https://meghasworldsite.wordpress.com and tweets at @meghasood16

CPSIA information can be obtained
at www.ICGtesting.com
Printed in the USA
LVHW090008100222
710541LV00022B/217